31 Day Devotional

For the Hearts of Estranged Mothers

Dorlene Smith

In Loving Memory

In loving memory of my Aunt Marcella James, she was a loving wife and mother who often encouraged me with these beautiful words, "No matter where a child goes…people will always want to know who their mother is." Gone too soon; rest in peace.

Published by Pen It! Publications, LLC in the United States of America
812-371-4128 www.penitpublications.com

ISBN: 978-1-951263-63-8
LIB # TXu 2…145-895
Edited by Cassy Cochrun

Dedication

This book is dedicated to my loving mother, Annie Lee Green. My mother is a faithful prayer warrior with a heart of gold. She was a registered nurse for 40 years before she retired in 2012. My mother has two children, eight grandchildren. God has blessed her with abundant wisdom, and she has shared that wisdom with her children. Whenever I need encouragement, my mom has always been there for me, and she is always praying for my success as a writer. Thank you, mom, for all of your prayers, I love you.

All glory and honor to you alone Jesus, my Lord and Savior! I will forever praise you for the song you gave to me in my night season. Thank you for all you have brought me through, because of you I am more than a conqueror!

Acknowledgements

I would like to say a special, "thank you," to my darling husband; He has the biggest heart. I could not have written this book without your never-ending support. You are my greatest fan! You instructed me, guided me and gave me serious and honest feedback; thank you. We loved each other through the pain and God has made us better for it. Thank you...I love you forever and ever.

Apostle, Doctor Jannie E. Brady...thanks for faithfully speaking the word of God into my life and constantly reminding me to keep writing; you always encouraged me to finish this book, you would motivate me to write, even if I did not feel like writing. You said to me "Faith is not about feeling, it is indeed an action."

Introduction

I lay on my living room floor with tears pouring out of my eyes. I asked the Lord, "Why am I still crying over this situation, which broke my heart?" The Lord answered me and said, "Because you are not healed" Not healed... I thought I was over it, after all two years had passed. I confessed that I had not dealt with the pain in my heart, but I had buried it deep. I am sure you have heard the phrase that time heals all wounds; I do not believe that is true. Time is not the healer; God is but He uses time to bring about healing. The first step toward healing is admitting that you are hurt. When we admit we are hurt, we are facing our pain and in facing our pain, we feel it, we can get through it. It does not matter how much time has gone by if we have not dealt with our pain, we are still wounded and in need of healing. If we bury our pain, we need to make sure it is dead first. If we try to bury our pain and it is not dead, it will come back kicking and screaming like a person being buried alive.

Our daughter made a decision that caused my husband and I great pain. She became estranged to us for fourteen years. Through no fault of our own, she chose to leave us. Our hearts were broken.

Many days and nights, tears were my food. Psalm 42:3.

My story of heartbreak is not so much about what happened to me as it is about what God did for me and through me. I think one of the greatest promises in the word of God is that, He promises to never leave nor forsake us.

The journey to healing began in the prayer room. I asked God to heal me. God's presence was my survival, and each day as I entered into His presence, I was strengthened a little more and a little more. In the prayer room I wrestled with the fact that I had no control over the situation I was facing. I could not make things be what I wanted them to be. I learned how to relinquish to God what I could not control.

We are strengthened and made by the things that are unpleasant, the things that break us and hurt us. Most of the time we never find out who we are or how much we can endure until, we go through a storm. I never knew I could withstand so much heartache, until I went through this storm. I never knew I could wait on God for so many years. In the storm, my identity was revealed, and I found out who I truly am... a warrior!

He alone is my safe place, His wrap – around presence always protects me as my champion defender. There's no risk of failure with God! So why should I let worry paralyze me, even when troubles multiply around me? God's glory is all around me His wrap around presence is all I need, for the Lord is my Savior, my hero, and my life- giving strength. Join me, everyone! Trust only in God every moment! Tell Him all your troubles and pour out your heart- longings to Him. Believe me when I tell you – He will help you! Psalm 62:6-8 TPT

Heartbreak

You are hurting so badly until you literally feel your heart breaking. You grip your chest—as if by doing so you could hold your heart into place—so your heart will not break into a million pieces. I was in the grocery store when I heard the words my daughter spoke; they broke my heart. A mother's heart can be as tough as steel and yet as tender as a grape.

Emergency personnel train regularly and are well prepared for any disaster or devastating event which life throws at them. When they arrive on scene, they quickly assess the situation, stabilize the wounded and work to prevent further injury. However, what mother is really prepared for her child to break her heart? There is no training program for that. There are some things in life that we cannot prepare for. I believe heartbreak is one of them.

You can trust that God's love will show up at the scene of your heartbreak and begin to repair the damage. He feels your pain and He knows exactly what to do about it. God will carefully assess your injury and take the appropriate actions. His love is patient, and His love is kind. He will calm and bring healing to your aching heart. If you are asking yourself, "How does she know this so well?" The answer is simple: I was once one of you.

Prayer

I am in an enormous amount of pain Father. Revive my heart with your powerful love so that I may not only survive this agonizing pain but grow from it as well.

Scripture

I've learned that His anger lasts for a moment, but his loving favor lasts a lifetime! We may weep through the night, but at daybreak it will turn into shouts of ecstatic joy. Psalm 30:5

Notes

_____

_____

_____

_____

_____

_____

_____

Hope

"How could my child do this to me?" Estranged parents have asked themselves this question, over and over, I know I did. "How in the world will I be able to cope?" You try to pinpoint the exact thing or things that have brought you to this gut-wrenching place. Your child, whom you love, has rejected you. Wishing you could go back in time, and prevent this horrible nightmare from happening, you plead with God to repair the relationship. You are feeling most weak; you need strength to avoid remaining in despair.

Each morning you awaken greeted by the undeniable wound of estrangement that is in your heart. Even though you are wounded, life keeps moving and it demands no less of you. What gets you up every morning and speaks to you, telling you to fight when you are tempted to lie in bed all day? It is hope! You must fight to hold on to hope that lies deep down within you. Hope compels us to live beyond our current circumstances; hope enables us to live beyond our pain.

With God, we can abound in hope! Hope is a powerful weapon, even if a tiny bit of it remains; it will be enough to strengthen us and pull us up out of despair. God will give us strength not just to face another day, but also to welcome each new day with expectation and hope.

Prayer

Father...when my days seem never ending, when my

mind fights me to dwell on my pain, help me to

embrace you...the God of all Hope.

Scripture

Now may God, the inspiration and fountain of

hope, fill you to overflowing with uncontainable

joy and perfect peace as you trust in Him. And

may the power of the Holy Spirit continually

surround your life with His super-abundance

until you radiate with hope! Romans 15:13

Notes

Broken Hearts

"Where do Broken Hearts Go" was the name of a song that the late Whitney Houston performed. The song asks a question of its listeners: "Where do broken hearts go?" After experiencing heartbreak, I realized that it was alright if my heart broke, God will gather up the broken pieces and put them all back into place.

The fragments of your broken heart are not to be discarded; as if they have no value or no purpose. God knows the worth of each piece of your shattered heart. Trust Him now to pick up the remnants of your broken heart; your broken dream and your broken expectations. Gathering one piece at a time, He [God] puts our broken hearts back together.

Do not fear a broken heart, for no matter where each piece falls, God sees it. Thank God for picking up all of your fragments because by doing so, He made your heart completely whole again. The answer to the aforementioned question, "Where do broken hearts go," is that they go to God for healing.

Prayer

Father, show me that even with my broken heart I can worship you, knowing that you will mend all the broken pieces.

Scripture

When you pass through the waters, I will be with you; And through the rivers, they shall not overflow you. When you walk through the fire, you shall not be burned, Nor shall the flame scorch you. Isaiah 43:2

Notes

Crushed

What do you do when you feel like the very essence of life has been drained out of you? Your pain is overwhelming, and tears are covering your face; you are in shock and disbelief. I almost dropped all the grocery I had in my arms...so I placed the items on the shelf right where I was standing. With one hand, I covered my heart and with the other hand, I covered my mouth--so I would not cry out in agony. Her words were like a dagger that pierced deep into my heart. Without hesitation, with my head hung low, I exited the store and ran to my car. I knew if I could just make it to my car, it would instantly become a temporary haven for my aching heart.

Sitting in my car feeling as if time was not the only thing that was frozen, but I felt frozen as well. I wondered in that moment; if I was going to even survive this situation, or even if I wanted to survive.

I cried on the way home, thinking about how my day began. When I awoke, the sun was shining brightly in my life, little did I know a storm was brewing and by noon, my day would turn completely dark. My heart had been crushed into tiny pieces and if not for God's love and strength, those pieces would have been lost forever.

God works immediately to help you endure the initial shock of heartbreak. When the shock wears off you will need Him, and He will be there. God will

never leave your side.

Prayer

Father when the pain I feel in my heart is crushing me, and I am falling apart, thank you that I can trust you to be there. There is no better place to fall apart than in your loving arms.

Scripture

The Lord is close to all whose hearts are crushed by pain, and he is always ready to restore the repentant one. Psalm 34:18

Notes

Forgiveness

Forgiveness is a journey that leads you to a place of freedom. Forgiveness is not for the benefit of the forgiven, but for the freedom of the forgiver. Until you forgive, forgive what your child did to you, you are stuck in a continuous feedback loop of pain. The enemy of your soul wants you to hold on to pain, experiencing it over and over again in your mind, never becoming free. Forgiving your child for the pain they caused is necessary for a new beginning. When there is unforgiveness in your heart, your love cannot flow. Unforgiveness blocks your love and it becomes pent-up; all whom you love suffer along with you. Unforgiveness will take on a life of its own consuming the life of the one who harbors it in their heart. Do not allow your love to become constrained; release any unforgiveness so that love can flow. God wants to bring forth the healing and wholeness, He has predestined for you. Serve notice to unforgiveness and tell it that your release date has come.

Prayer

Father, I have been clutching unforgiveness so tight,

and I do not know how to let it go. By faith right

now, I release all unforgiveness so that I may sow a

seed for new beginnings in my life today. Amen.

Scripture

Therefore, if the Son makes you free, you shall

be free indeed. John 8:36

Notes

Acceptance

When your relationship with your child has been broken, accepting this fact is one of the hardest things you will ever do. For a long time, I refused to accept the truth; I did not want to believe that I was a mother who was estranged from her child. Until I accepted that truth, I was keeping myself from grieving and from healing. I could not ignore the pain that was in my heart...no matter how hard I tried. It seemed like everywhere I went I would see mothers out with their daughters and enjoying their relationship. I was reminded of my painful reality; that I did not have what I was longing for...my daughter. Accepting what has happened between you and your child does not automatically bring forth change, but recognizing the reality is the first step toward change. The first step is usually the most difficult one, but you do not have to take it alone.

Denying your pain keeps you living in the past; that is not God's will. Letting go of what you think should have been frees you to live in the present and look forward to your future. Yes, I did say your future, because you still have one. Just as the breaking forth of a river, from the confines of a dam, moves everything in the torrents path...acceptance will bring forth a flood of emotions. Acceptance clears the path for healing!

Prayer

Father, I have denied the pain long enough; I want to be free. Help me not to focus on what should have been, but to focus on you and the good that is to come from your steadfast love. Thank you for my change.

Amen.

Scripture

I look up to the mountains and hills, longing for God's help. But then I realize that our true help and protection come only from the Lord, our Creator who made the heavens and the earth.

Psalm 121:1-2

Notes

_____

_____

_____

_____

_____

_____

_____

Where Are You Going?

The first work of reconciliation, which God performs, is right in your own heart.

Hagar ran away from Sarai when she dealt harshly with her. And he [God's angel] said, "Hagar, slave of Sarai, where have you come from, and where are you going?" "I'm running away from my mistress Sarai," she answered. Then the angel of the LORD said to her, "Return to your mistress, and submit yourself to her authority."... Genesis 16:8-9.

God always requires you to stop running, go back, and face what you are running from. Running did not work for Hagar and it is not going to work for you. Strength does not come from running but from standing. God will teach you how to stand. Just remember, when you are standing, you are not alone. Running away from your pain appears to be easier. God knows that running away from pain, solves nothing; it only delays healing. If you are going to run, then run to Him.

Prayer

Father your word teaches me to stand and to be strong

in you. Help me to face my pain and not run away.

Thank you for always standing with me. Amen.

Scripture

The name of the Lord is a strong tower; the

righteous run to it and are safe. Proverbs 18:10

Notes

Am I Forgotten?

Questions bombard your mind...day in and day out.

Questions such as, "Do they even care?" "Do they think about me at all?" "Are they going through pain as well?" "Did they forget that they have a family?" "How could my child so easily drop me and move on with their life?" These are questions that, you never thought you would ever have to face. Each question makes the hole in your heart a little deeper. Finally, you ask yourself, "Am I forgotten?"

The loneliness that is within your heart makes you feel forgotten even abandoned. Let me try to reassure you that you matter, and you are always on the heart of the heavenly Father.

In the midst of all your concerns, quickly and compassionately, God responds to your question loudly and clearly "No, you are not forgotten, nor will you ever be."

Prayer:

Father when the questions come, when I am looking

for answers, help me to proclaim boldly in my heart,

"I am not forgotten!" Amen.

Scripture

Can a woman forget her nursing child,

and not have compassion on the son of her

womb? Surely, they may forget, See, I have

inscribed you on the palms of My hands; Yet I

will not forget you. Your walls are continually

before Me. Isaiah 49:15-16

Notes

_____

_____

_____

_____

_____

_____

_____

Shame

The shame that you feel, being an estranged parent,

is not easy to share. You try to keep all of your pain,

what it has done to you, bottled up inside. The

embarrassment that you feel keeps you from reaching

out for help. You would rather not talk about your

child; you prefer to keep your pain private. When you

are conversing with others and the subject of your

child eventually comes up, you tend to struggle for

the right words to say; words that will guard against

exposing your afflicted heart. The friend, who does

not know your situation, innocently asks, "When is

your child going to visit?" Family members, who do not know the depth of your estrangement, question you; they want answers that you just do not have. Estrangement is a secret pain, a weight borne by many mothers and fathers, often suffered in silence.

Find the courage to expose the hurt and shame; it feels like it is the worst thing that you could possibly do, but it is not. Shame is a painful feeling of humiliation or distress caused by the consciousness of wrong or foolish behavior. Shame is a powerful emotion that eats you up on the inside. God's love will give you the strength to talk about your pain. God knows the hurt of shame; He will free you completely. God's love is the antidote for all shame.

Prayer

Father the shame I feel causes me to hang my head down. I have tried to keep my shame hidden and locked up in my heart, and it is consuming me from the inside. I ask you to free me by your grace and help me to lift up my head and walk in your love. Amen.

Scripture

Instead of your shame you shall have double honor, and instead of confusion they shall rejoice in their portion. Therefore, in their land they shall possess double; Everlasting joy shall be theirs. Isaiah 61:7

Notes

Bitterness

When the enemy comes along and offers bitterness, do not take it, it is poison. The bible cautions us with regard to the root of bitterness and warns us not to be defiled by it. Bitterness corrupts our heart and gives us a false comfort. When we are bitter, everything that comes from us is bitter as well. Bitterness only begets more bitterness. Bitterness, if allowed to persist in our lives, spreads outward and it defiles all that it touches. The longer we remain bitter, the deeper the root of it will grow...right down to the very core of our being.

Bitterness is invited into our lives when un-forgiveness is allowed to remain. We invite bitterness in when we do not release our pain. A hard heart is the offspring of bitterness. Do not be deceived by the root of bitterness. In the end, bitterness will turn on us, if we allow it to stay, and devour us utterly. At one point, I was tempted to open the door to bitterness and invite it to dwell in me. The enemy spoke to me and said, "Turn down every picture that you have of your daughter...she is dead to you." The enemy's ultimate goal is to kill and destroy families; mother-daughter relationships, father-son relationships...it does not matter. God's love protects our hearts from becoming bitter. I declared to the enemy, that day,

"There is no room in my heart for bitterness, but only for God's love."

Prayer

Father let your love fill my heart and overflow. When I am hurting, please help me to choose love over bitterness; this I cannot do on my own. Amen.

Scripture

So above all, guard the affections of your heart, for they affect all that you are.

Pay attention to the welfare of your innermost being, for from there flows the wellspring of life.

Proverbs 4:23

Notes

Scarred Heart

A Scar is a mark that remains as the visible evidence of a healed wound. Not all scars are visible to the naked eye. For example, when someone has suffered a heart attack, there are scars that form in the heart muscle, because of the infarction. There are mothers walking around with a scarred heart due to a traumatic separation between them and their children. There is no doubt that this type of hurt, experienced by mothers, can leave them scarred for life. The scars they have, both seen, and unseen can be reminders of God's love, and how He has healed them.

God will use the pain and the scars which you have endured to bring forth a new and stronger mother. We are often ashamed of our scars, our hurts, so we try to cover them up. We cover them [our hurts] with pretend smiles, hoping that no one will notice them. Scarring is a natural part of the healing process. Your scars are indicators that you are surviving, and God is going to make you thrive again; wear them as a badge of honor. His love never fails; His love heals, and it never stops working.

Prayer

Father, thank you for my scars; those that cannot be

seen, you see. I do not have to be self-conscious about

my scars, but I can testify that I have overcome in

spite of them.

Scripture

Lord! I'm bursting with joy over what you've

done for me! My lips are full of perpetual praise.

Psalm 34:1

Notes

Helplessness

What does a mother do with the helplessness that she feels perched over her, threatening to crush her, waiting for her to crumble? I wanted to do something, anything, to keep the relationship between my daughter and me from being destroyed. I agonized over the powerless feelings that seem to immobilize me. Helplessness places one in a vulnerable position, being unable to do anything to make their situation better…or easier.

I dropped to my knees and said, "God I am weak" and He said, "I [God] am strong; allow my power to reign supreme within you." When we confess our weakness, we are confessing our dependence on God; that makes us strong. I felt God's love embracing me; I knew, in that moment, nothing and no one could do me any harm. I declared, "I am helped!

Prayer

Father you are my strength when I am feeling helpless. Help me to confess my weakness so that your power can make me strong. Amen.

Scripture

Beat your plowshares into swords, and your pruning hooks into spears; let the weak say, I am strong. Joel 3:10

Notes

To Compensate or Not to Compensate

When the heart is unable to pump enough blood throughout the body, the resulting condition is referred to as "heart failure." The heart begins to make up for the lack of pumping efficiency by enlarging itself. An enlarged heart places greater demands on the body. You can be in heart failure for years, without having any idea, because the heart is great at counterpoising. The heart is an amazing muscle, but it cannot compensate indefinitely; inevitably, the adverse effects of the damaged heart will be manifested.

How many times have you tried to make up for the emptiness and the pain in your heart? When you compensate for pain and heartache, it is only a temporary fix; you will do more harm to yourself than good. People tend to compensate in many ways, especially when they are hurting.

Some mothers become workaholics, and some engage in social activities, but I dealt with my pain by pretending I did not care. I kept my love and emotions on the inside. God showed me that I needed to feel the pain in my heart in order to receive my healing. To feel your pain is to face your pain; when you face it, you can get through it. Compensation may help you to cope at first, but it does not fix anything; all it does is mask your pain.

Prayer

Father, please help me to face the pain in my heart head on. Help me to realize that every temporary fix is just that, temporary. Amen.

Scripture

Though we experience every kind of pressure, we're not crushed. At times we don't know what to do, but quitting is not an option. We are persecuted by others, but God has not forsaken us. We may be knocked down, but not out. 2 Corinthians 4:8-9

Notes

Rejection

Rejection can be extremely painful, especially when it comes from someone you love. To be constantly subjected to rejection can affect your sense of self-worth and everything that makes you who you are. So many times, I tried to reach out to my daughter...hoping she would receive me. I felt like she was the one who could bring comfort and relief to my tormented heart. I thought if she would just accept me, I could move on and despite the hurt, everything would be okay. Unfortunately, life is not that simple; I was wounded, and I needed healing. My pleas for her love and acceptance went unanswered and I asked myself, "What is wrong with me…am I not good enough?"

Worthiness is rooted in Christ and no one else. I am good enough and you are good enough. You matter to God, and He will take away the emptiness and rejection you feel. "He who created you, Jacob, he who formed you, Israel: Do not fear, for I have redeemed you; I have summoned you by name; you are mine" (Isaiah 43:1).

Prayer

Father, the rejection that I feel has ripped me to my core. Help me to soak in your love, because it will heal my heart. Amen.

Scripture

For the Lord will never walk away from his cherished ones, nor would he forsake his chosen ones who belong to him. Psalm 94:14

Notes

Sleepless Nights

When I think of heartbreak, I think of Joseph; he had to live with unfathomable hurt and disappointment from his family. Joseph was rejected and hated by his own brothers. There can be no doubt that the pain he endured had to bring him many sleepless nights. Even more consequential is the fact that he spent those sleepless nights in prison. Some of those nights were likely filled with tears, because he loved his family. In the midst of those long nights, in which daybreak seemed to never appear, God was there. Every sleepless night you have had, thinking of your son…thinking of your daughter, God has recorded.

Physically…you are on the brink of exhaustion; your spirit, mind and body need rest. Remember that the battle is not yours, but it is the Lord's. God is going to turn things around for you, so that you will be able to declare like the Psalmist King David, "…for He grants sleep to those he loves."

Prayer

Father, thank you for your anointing to sleep in the midst of the storm. Help me to relinquish all of my restless thoughts, for I know daybreak is on the way.

Amen.

Scripture

Now, because of you, Lord, I will lie down in peace and sleep comes at once, for no matter what happens, I will live unafraid! Psalm 4:8

Notes

Letting Go

Dealing with fearful thoughts, worrying about your child, has worn you down; their absence has changed your world forever. Time is gradually changing you, changing your perspective. That perfect picture, you know...the one you have in mind of your child returning, is fading. You are beginning to realize that you cannot live a broken life.

Perhaps you are thinking, "If I let go of the pain, I will lose the connection I feel with my child," despite the fact that they are physically gone. Love is the everlasting bond; it cannot be broken no matter how far they roam. Releasing your child can free you from the emotional pain; giving you the courage to go on with your life. Your relationship with your child may never be the same, but it can be better, closer and even stronger. Release both your child and your pain to God; He will paint a brand-new picture for you. God is watching and He will take care of you both.

Prayer

Father it feels like letting go is giving up on my child.

Help me to realize that when I let go, I let you.

Amen.

Scripture

The LORD gives strength to His people; the LORD will bless His people with peace. Psalm 29:11

Notes

The Waiting Factor

There were days that I struggled with waiting; I needed God to heal my anguished heart. In order to wait on God, I had to put my complete trust in Him. When you become weary from waiting, the best things to do is worship. Worship draws you in to a deeper realm of faith, and a deeper realm or rest. In times of trouble and disappointment, you can draw closer to God; you draw nearer through worship.

Waiting on God is synonymous with trusting God. If you are going to wait on God, you must trust

Him and if you are going to trust Him then you must wait on Him; you cannot have one without the other.

While you are waiting on God, He is doing a great and valuable work in you; He is laying the groundwork for a strong faith. Between the waiting and fulfillment, there is a whole lot of changing going on inside of you. God will not waste one ounce of your pain, but He will use it to help bring hope and healing to others.

Prayer

Father, waiting seems to be so hard for me to do.

Help me to draw closer to you through my worship.

When I become impatient, strengthen me, in order

that I may hold fast, so that I can enter into a deeper

place of worship. Amen.

Scripture

But those who wait on the LORD shall
renew their strength; they shall mount up with
wings like eagles, they shall run and not be
weary, they shall walk and not faint. Isaiah 40:31

Notes

In God's Recovery Room

The recovery room is where you are taken after you have been wounded, suffered a traumatic injury or endured a surgery, either major or minor, for recuperation. One of the main goals of your health care team is to make sure that your body recovers from the procedure. In the recovery room, your heart rate, breathing, and blood pressure are closely monitored. The room is equipped with highly advanced equipment, which is ready to be used if needed. The recovery room is not intended for an extended stay. Once you have awakened and you are out of danger, you will be moved into a personal room. Hopefully, in a reasonable amount of time, you will regain your strength and be able to check out and go home.

When you have suffered spiritual, mental or emotional wounds, you need to recover; God's presence is your recovery room. God never leaves your side and you can rest knowing that you are in the best of hands: God's hands!

Prayer

Father thank you for your presence, that restores me and bring me to a state of perfect health. I know that I am in the best of hands and I will recover all.

Amen.

Scripture

So, David inquired at the LORD, saying, "Shall I pursue this troop? Shall I overtake them?" And He answered him, "Pursue, for you shall surely overtake them and without fail recover all." I Samuel 30:8

Notes

The Power of Worship

God's mercy overcomes all shame and fear, for He says, "I am the Lord: for they shall not be ashamed [disappointed] that wait for me" (Isaiah 49:24). Worship places you on the path to healing. The pain of estrangement can bring your life to a screeching halt. However, by worshiping, you can "live" in the midst of your heartbreak. The enemy wants you to surrender your faith, but your faith fuels your worship! Worship carries you into God's presence. You can create an atmosphere of worship in the midst of any situation. Worship is a door that is capable of keeping love and faith locked securely in

your heart and keeping doubt locked completely out.

Prayer

Father thank you for the gift of worship. I am so humbled that you have given me the privilege to worship you. Teach me to worship you with every breath until all my fears and shame are gone. Amen.

Scripture

Never doubt God's mighty power to work in you and accomplish all this. He will achieve infinitely more than your greatest request, your most unbelievable dream, and exceed your wildest imagination! He will outdo them all, for his miraculous power constantly energizes you.

Ephesians 3: 20-21

Notes

_____

_____

_____

_____

_____

_____

_____

_____

Victims

When a separation between parents and their children takes place, the grandchildren, if there are any, are potential innocent victims. Grandparents are frequently cut off from their grandchildren; this is a very distressing consequence of the estrangement. My heart ached for a relationship with my grandchildren.

I was not present for the birth of any of my daughter's six beautiful children; missing their births was not my choice. My grandchildren knew neither myself nor their grandfather. My husband and I desperately wanted to have a relationship with our grandchildren and share with them all of our love. God blessed us with two more beautiful grandchildren through our son and his wife. We were able to be there for their entrance into the world. I thank God every day for the opportunity to witness such special miracles. If your grandchildren are estranged from you, I know your pain; just remember God is a God of justice.

Prayer

Father I thank you that you are a God of Justice. My grandchildren are a gift from you, and I ask you to bless my life with their presence... Amen.

Scripture

Therefore, the Lord will wait, that He may be gracious to you; And therefore, He will be exalted, that He may have mercy on you. For the Lord is a God of justice; Blessed are all those who wait for Him. Isaiah 30:18

Notes

Anger

Do not hold on to anger; it is most certainly a terrible caretaker. Some view anger as a comforter; holding onto it makes them feel better. Not releasing the anger allows them to avoid the inevitable pain of dealing with issues that caused the anger in the first place. Anger will not take care of you; it will destroy your life. Remaining angry requires an immense expenditure of energy. It is a much better use of your energy to focus it on taking care of the family that remains with you. Anger drains your strength and leads you away from your healing, not towards it. If anger remains, you cannot be healed. If you make anger a foundation, everything that you place on top of it can come crashing down in an instant; at any moment you could be left broken and shattered again.

Prayer

Father please help me to let go of my anger and walk

in your peace and healing. Amen.

Scripture

The Lord God is in your midst, The Mighty

One, will save; He will rejoice over you with

gladness, He will quiet you with His love, He

will rejoice over you with singing. Zephaniah

3:17

Notes

_____

_____

_____

_____

_____

_____

_____

_____

Fear

Fear would have you do nothing, once the heart has been deeply hurt; it shudders to think of ever feeling that pain again. I feared my other child would walk out of my life. The fear of loss is real, and it can cause you to cling tighter to whatever you have left. You keep your other children close and pour all of yourself into them. If you have no other children, then you pour into yourself. Whatever I did was based on the fear of loss. I would not do something or do more of something just to appease my fears.

Fear is not love; in fact, the bible says that "There is no fear in love; but perfect love casts out fear, because fear involves torment. But he who fears has not been made perfect in love" (I John 4:18). My mind was plagued daily with thoughts of losing my son. I had to make a choice, it was either fear or faith, but one would cancel out the other. If I was to walk in faith, I had to trust that whatever happened, God would bless me to conquer it. "For I am persuaded that neither death nor life, nor angels nor principalities nor powers, nor things present nor things to come, nor height nor depth, nor any other created thing, shall be able to separate us from the love of God which is in Christ Jesus our Lord" (Romans 8:38-39).

Prayer

Father when fear is trying to overtake my mind by filling it with thoughts of what ifs, I thank you that your word reassures me that nothing will be able to separate me from your love. I know your love will take care of everything that concerns me.

Scripture

God has not given us a spirit of fear but of power, love, and a sound mind. 2 Timothy 1:7

Notes

Keep Sowing

Do not give up hope concerning your child. I planted flowers in my front yard, some of which would not grow. I became so frustrated that I was ready to snatch them out of the ground. The following morning, I noticed the flowers, which had not bloomed yet, suddenly had tiny petals on them. In my haste and impatience, I could have destroyed my flowers. Do not be so quick to pull up what you have sown (i.e., prayers, tears, etc.); God sees all, and He can detect the smallest amount of change in your situations. Be patient and continue to trust God, knowing that the harvest you are waiting for will come to fruition.

Prayer

Father I have been waiting and waiting for my change to come; please help me not to give up. Amen.

Scripture

He has made everything beautiful in its time.

Ecclesiastes 3:11

Notes

_____

_____

_____

_____

_____

_____

_____

Cleaning the Wound

Without forgiveness, there can be no healing. Unforgiveness keeps our wounds open and an open wound puts us at risk for infection. Forgiveness cleanses our hearts and sanitizes our wounds so that healing can begin. If we allow our hearts to become infected, the infection will spread not only in our own lives but also throughout our whole family. Cleaning the wound is the most painful part and most necessary to assure proper healing.

Prayer

Father as painful as it may be, help me to forgive so that my heart can be cleansed and healed. Amen.

Scripture

Love is large and incredibly patient. Love is gentle and consistently kind to all. It refuses to be jealous when blessing comes to someone else. Love does not brag about one's achievements nor inflate its own importance. Love does not traffic in shame and disrespect, nor selfishly seek its own honor. Love is not easily irritated or quick to take offense. Love joyfully celebrates honesty and finds no delight in what is wrong. Love is a safe place of shelter, for it never stops believing the best for others. Love never takes failure as defeat, for it never gives up. I Corinthians 13: 4-8

111

Notes

Through the Valley

When your heart is heavy and hurting, give God the praise. The ability to exalt God, while you are hurting, is within your capability. In spite of your suffering, God has not changed. He is who He is; He is perfect, and He is just. He will walk with you through your valley.

There comes a time when your journey though extremely difficult becomes easier and easier; you begin to recognize you have the power to endure without breaking. Your future...and the future of your child are in God's hands; there is no need to worry.

Your faith has helped you completely surrender all your pain to God. You can boast in God and declare "My God has come through!"

Prayer

Father, thank you for walking with me through my valley. I will not worry at all, but I will boast in your goodness. Amen.

Scripture

Pour out all your worries and stress upon him and leave them there, for he always tenderly cares for you. Psalm 34:1.

Notes

_____

_____

_____

_____

_____

_____

_____

Keeping an Open Heart

How do you make it through a broken heart? How do you get through a wounded spirit without bitterness? You get through it [a broken heart] on your knees. You can get through anything on your knees. Prayer is an essential key to keeping your aching heart open; an open heart is crucial to healing. You cannot allow pain to close your heart; doing so establishes a barrier that will prevent you from moving forward. The only way to move forward...is on your knees. You cannot bare the heaviness of a sorrowful heart alone. When you take your grieving heart to God in prayer, it will be strengthened. The hurt in your heart, in time, will begin to diminish slowly. With hope, you will be able to look to the future again.

Prayer

Father I thank you for an open heart so that I may

continue to move forward in love. Amen.

Scripture

Continue earnestly in prayer, being vigilant in it

with thanksgiving... Colossians 4:2

Notes

Joy

There are so many moments in our lives when we forget to enjoy what God has given to us. In times of great suffering and pain, we can fail to remember how to appreciate life. Life does not seem like something to celebrate in dark times, but it is the spark of joy that can set everything else ablaze in our lives. In the moments that we find ourselves laughing about something, right in the midst of our misery, we are reminded that love conquers heartbreak, laughter conquers tears and faith defeats our fears. God says, "I will turn your sorrow into joy." The very thing that has made you sorry...God will use to bring you joy!

For He knows the way that you take and when you

are tried, you shall come forth as pure gold.

Prayer

Father thank you that we don't have to drown in our tears, but we can have joy again. Teach us how to appreciate life in trying times. Amen.

Scripture

Do not sorrow, for the joy of the Lord is your strength. Nehemiah 8:10

Notes

_____

_____

_____

_____

_____

_____

_____

Restoration

Restoration is to bring back into a state of health.

When you think of good health, what usually comes to mind is the condition of your body. However, health refers to not only the state of your body, but also just as importantly the state of your mind. Your mind, your emotions and intellect, have a direct effect on how your body performs. Depression for example is a mental state, which, if left untreated, can affect your body. When God says, "I will restore your health," He means the whole you: mind, body and soul.

There are healthcare professionals who specialize in treating different parts of your body; God specializes in the total being. Whether the problem is physical, mental or spiritual...God specializes! You have the greatest physician and He promises to restore you to health!

Prayer

Father I thank you that restoration time has come.

Restore every part of my life; make me whole again.

Amen.

Scripture

For I will restore health to you and heal you of your wounds; says the LORD... Jeremiah 30:17

Notes

Love

One day, the house that I live in turned dark, and it stayed that way for a long time. My house was dark because I closed all the blinds and refused to let any light in. My pain had taken me to a dark place; I was held captive there. Pain was my dungeon. Love was there with me in my dungeon at all times; I did not speak to love but love spoke to me. I did not care for love, but love cared for me. Love changed me and called me out of my prison. Love took me by the hand and walked me out of my cell. Love opened the blinds of my house and the light shinned through. No longer do I cry for your love; I know I am loved. No longer

do I wait for you to change, because I am changed.

When I think of you, I think, "you are mine and you

always will be." Just as love took care of me, I asked

love to take care of you...Love Mom.

Prayer

Father I thank you that I am neither a prisoner of my pain nor a prisoner to my past, but I am freed by your love. Amen.

Scripture

For the Lord is good; His mercy is everlasting, And His truth endures to all generations.

Psalm 100:5

Notes

_____

_____

_____

_____

_____

_____

_____

Motherhood

Motherhood is sacred; it is a God ordained calling.

It is a lifelong call. The fact that your child has left does not negate your call as a Mother. No one can take the gift of motherhood away from you. No matter where your child goes, someone will always want to know, "who is your mother?"

Do you remember the first prayer you uttered to God for your child? Your prayer probably went something like this: "God, please bless my child to be healthy and help me to be a good mother...Amen." God still remembers that prayer, so trust that He is

helping you right now. I am who I am, and that is a
Mother.

Prayer

Father, thank you for the calling of Motherhood. I am confident that you don't make mistakes. You made me a Mother and I will forever be a Mother. Amen.

Scripture

So now we come freely and boldly to where love is enthroned, to receive mercy's kiss and discover the grace we urgently need to strengthen us in our time of weakness.

Hebrews 4:16

Notes

Promises

I am healed...and the pain of my once broken heart plagues me no more. Pain was my assailant for so long, but now it is dead and buried; I am free! My relationship with my child is mending and I am rejoicing every day for what God has done. I had to learn how to rejoice, even when I felt like I had no reason to do so. God taught me, in the middle of my pain, how to persevere and to hold on to His promises. His [God's] promises became my reason to rejoice. God loves our children and He gives us His assurance that He will not cease from following our children; He will do them good (Jeremiah 32:41). The road of estrangement is paved with the tears of mothers and fathers. I do not know where your road will lead you, but God promises He will work it out for your good.

Prayer

Father thank you for your promises in your unfailing word. Your word is the rock on which I stand; all other ground is sinking sand. Amen.

Scripture

And so, we are convinced that every detail of our lives is continually woven together to fit into God's perfect plan of bringing good into our lives, for we are his lovers who have been called to fulfill his designed purpose. Romans 8:28

Notes

Author Dorlene Elizabeth Smith is married to the love of her life Charles M. Smith Sr.; they have shared 31 wonderful years of love. Dorlene and her husband reside in Charleston South Carolina; they have two children and eight lovely grandchildren. Dorlene has been volunteering for 4 years as a counselor at a local Pregnancy Center in her community. Ministering to and helping women of all ages is her passion. She enjoys visiting their grandchildren and riding with her husband on his motorcycle. Her husband is a retired Marine with over 20 years of honorable and faithful service. He is currently a Registered Radiation Therapist who treats cancer patients in the Oncology Department of one of the local hospitals.

CPSIA information can be obtained
at www.ICGtesting.com
Printed in the USA
BVHW071606021219
565404BV00021B/3130/P